Some of the original paintings in this book are available as fine art prints.
For information on purchasing prints or award-winning books,
or to request a free Noël Studio color catalog, contact:

The Sanctuary, The Art of N.A. Noël
75 North Main Street
Zionsville, Indiana 46077
317-733-1117 · 1-800-444-6635
www.nanoel.com

# JOY IN SIMPLICITY
*Creative Cooking with Artist Nancy Noël*

*The Art of Fresh, Fast and Fabulous Food*

*with Donna Deardorff*

Paintings by N. A. Noël
Research and recipes by N. A. Noël and Donna Deardorff
Design by Jennifer Bradley-Simmons
Layout assistance by Pam Fraizer
Editing by Lisa Rice Wheeler

PRINTED IN COLLABORATION WITH

*The Art of Fresh, Fast and Fabulous Food*

# JOY IN SIMPLICITY

*Creative Cooking with Artist Nancy Noël*

This book is dedicated to Rosie, who was born in Denmark. She came to America and devoted her life to cooking for my grandparents. Her example of what was truly good from the kitchen formed my critical palate. She was kind and patient and diligent. Her diligence led to perfection in the kitchen.

## My challenge has been to find that perfection without having to employ exceptional patience.

Often in describing a talented artist, the word finesse comes to mind. Rosie created her culinary masterpieces using finesse as the main ingredient.

—NANCY NOËL

# When it comes to cooking, my mantra is, "It shouldn't take longer to make it than it does to eat it."

For some, the idea of a perfect weekend or free afternoon would be baking cookies, cakes and pies, or preparing a feast for family and friends. Entertaining friends is one thing; however, endless preparation for the sheer pleasure of it is not for me. My enthusiasm for an all-day marathon in the kitchen would wane to "short order." When it comes to cooking, my mantra is, "It shouldn't take longer to make it than it does to eat it."

I never really considered myself a cook. I had to rethink this, as frequent visitors and guests repeatedly rave and request my recipes. They are amazed at just how easy they are to prepare.

Most cookbooks are written and designed for educated cooks. They often describe lengthy, complicated recipes with unfamiliar ingredients that can be difficult to find. I believe that a simple recipe often tastes better than a more complicated one.

In *Joy in Simplicity* you will find simple, healthy, delicious recipes using well-known, accessible and easy-to-find ingredients to create dishes that everyone will ask for. We have also included a health information section to aid in making educated choices.

In this cookbook, you will not find casseroles with potato chips or sausage, recipes with margarine or a base of processed or prepared foods. You will find healthy, easy-to-prepare, versatile recipes for all occasions and everyday cooking.

My serious interest in health began when I realized that my food awareness would influence for a lifetime the health and habits of my two sons. Before too long, junk food became taboo in our household along with most prepared and processed foods. The more I knew, the more proactive I became. I wanted to help others understand food and how, especially in these over-processed times, it could profoundly affect our lives, and that good eating and good health can go hand in hand...or hand to mouth.

Many thanks to Donna Deardorff, a natural health consultant, a wise and patient friend, and my favorite cook. Her research and her contributed recipes provide vital information for the everyday cook.

*by Nancy Noël*

Nancy paints by her pond on her 40-acre farm. Nancy's farm has been organic for over 20 years.

# Essentials for Creative Cooking

## Pantry

Olive Oil
Coconut Oil
Cooking Wine
Cooking Sherry
Balsamic Vinegar
Apple Cider Vinegar
Basil Oil
Lemon Oil
Stevia
Rapadura™ Sugar

## Freezer

Pecans
Pine Nuts

## Spices

Cumin
Coarse Black Pepper
Ginger
Fennel Seed
Sea Salt
Cajun Spice
Bay Leaves

## Refrigerator

Sour Cream
Heavy Whipping Cream
Eggs
Butter
Lemons
Limes
Red and White Onions
Real Mayonnaise
Wasabi Mayonnaise
Hot Sauce
Goat Feta Cheese

## Fresh Herbs

Cilantro
Dill
Oregano
Parsley
Basil
Tarragon
Chives
Garlic Cloves

**Note from Nancy**

- Wasabi mayonnaise is fabulous with so many foods. Try it on vegetables, fish and sandwiches.
- Sea salt makes a big difference in the taste of your food.
- I sauté pine nuts and keep them in my refrigerator. They are wonderful on salads and give almost any dish an added nutty flavor.
- Hot sauce adds spark to everything from eggs to soup.
- Goat feta is one of my favorite cheeses on almost everything. Try it in eggs, cole slaw, or wild rice.
- Stevia is a perfect way to almost eliminate sugar from your diet. I use it in coffee, tea, milk, fruit sauces and even in cole slaw.

1.   BASIL: Basil is one of the most commonly used herbs in cooking. The sweet odor of the fresh leaves makes them ideal for salads, soups, vegetables and tomato dishes. Basil is the main ingredient in pesto.

2.   CHIVES: Chives have a delicate onion flavor and sometimes can be substituted for green onions. They are commonly used with sour cream and in quiches, fish and soup recipes. Great on everything.

3.   CILANTRO: Cilantro is related to the parsley family. It has a pungent odor and is widely used in Asian, Caribbean and Mexican cooking. It is most commonly used in making salsa. Delicious with a variety of foods.

4.   CUMIN: Cumin has many antioxidant properties. According to research, the spice contains several pain-relieving compounds. I use cumin in almost all my chilies and soups.

5.   CURRY: Curry is a blend of spices and is used widely in dishes throughout India and Southeast Asia.

6.   DILL: Dill is best known for making pickles and its refreshing aroma. Sour cream is an ideal companion for fresh dill.

7.   FENNEL: Fennel is a versatile herb for cooking. The seeds, bulbs, leaves and flowers can all be used. I use fennel seeds in my grilled chicken salad recipe, which gives it an unusual flavor.

8.   GARLIC: Garlic is one most widely used herbs in cooking due to its strong flavor. Garlic is also believed to have medicinal uses. It is thought to stimulate the immune system and may be helpful in treating high blood pressure, asthma and diabetes.

9.   OREGANO: Oregano is often referred to as the pizza and spaghetti herb. In addition to tomato dishes, oregano can be used in bean salads, vegetables and soups. The leaves can either be used fresh or dried, depending upon the recipe.

10.   PARSLEY: Parsley is a widely used herb. Do not under estimate its subtle flavor. Many soup and salad recipes call for parsley, which is best used fresh. Most people are familiar with parsley only as a garnish.

11.   TARRAGON: Tarragon enhances the flavor of foods such as chicken, fish and cheese.

# Table of Contents

A variety of cookbooks collect dust on my kitchen shelf. This is not to say that I am a poor housekeeper; rather, like most everyday cooks, I fantasize about broadening my cooking portfolio. The reality is, however, that I keep going back to the recipes that are—and we all have them—tried and true. I have included for you the meals, and even the snacks, that I can never get enough of, and that never fail to garner raves from family and friends.

## I hope this book will complement the way you live and will make your life easier, more interesting and informed.

We've all done it: Buy the book, take it home, use it once or maybe not at all.  On a few occasions, I have tried some recipes only to be disappointed and astonished that they found their way into print. To make sure that doesn't happen when you use *Joy in Simplicity*, I have included the best basics along with quick, easy and flexible recipes. And to help you feed yourself and your family well every day, there's a reference section about commonly used foods and health.

—NANCY NOËL

We hope that most of your meals include a trip through the garden—an organic one. The following recipes are a selection of cold soups, a variety of salads and salsa. Remember, most of the recipes welcome creative change based on your personal taste.

## Pear Salsa

**Serves 10 to 12**
Recipe by Kristy Wells

2 large cans petite tomatoes, diced

4 tablespoons lime juice

1 large pear, finely chopped

1/2 purple onion, diced

1 to 2 jalapenos, diced

1/2 cup fresh cilantro, minced

2 to 4 teaspoons garlic, minced

1 teaspoons cumin

Salt and pepper to taste (easy on the salt)

Mix all ingredients together and refrigerate 1 hour before serving. Serve with plain or flavored chips of your choice.

**Note from Nancy**

This great unusual-tasting salsa was sent to us especially for our cookbook. The Noël Staff had a pitch-in to try new recipes and this was voted a great hit.

# Bruschetta

2 ripe tomatoes, chopped

1 avocado, chopped

1/2 cup goat feta cheese, crumbled

FINELY CHOP

2 tablespoons fresh oregano

2 tablespoons fresh basil

2 garlic cloves

Chop red onion to taste (optional)

MIX

Juice of 1/2 fresh lemon

2 or 3 tablespoons olive oil

6 slices of Tuscan-style bread

Combine all ingredients except bread in serving bowl. Drizzle bread with olive oil and broil until slightly brown. Spoon bruschetta on toasted bread. Serve warm.

There are many variations on bruschetta. Be creative. Also, goat cheese or cream cheese can be spread on bread.

# Tomato Basil Soup

**Serves 10**
Recipe by Keltie Domina

Butter

1 cup yellow onions, chopped

1 cup celery, chopped

3 cups fresh basil, chopped

1/2 cup sugar (optional)

2 tablespoons chicken base or

2 cups chicken stock

4 to 5 cups fresh tomatoes

4 to 5 cups tomato sauce

(use equal amounts of each)

1 cup sour cream

Melt butter in a large sauce pan, then add onion, celery and basil. After onions are translucent, add 1/2 cup of sugar and cook for about 5 minutes. (Sugar is optional; however, it does add a sweeter, richer taste.) Add 2 tablespoons chicken base (or 2 cups chicken stock) and 2 cups water.

Then add all tomato products and simmer on stove for about 15 to 30 minutes.

Just prior to serving add 1 cup sour cream and puree. Add salt, pepper and garlic salt to taste.

---

# Cold Cucumber Soup

**Serves 10**

4 cucumbers, peeled and seeded

2 bunches green onions, cleaned

1 pint sour cream

Salt, white pepper and garlic powder to taste

1 quart buttermilk

Juice of one lemon

Chopped parsley

Combine cucumbers and green onions in a processor or blender and puree until smooth. Transfer to a large bowl and whisk in sour cream and seasonings. Add buttermilk and lemon juice. Mix and chill overnight to develop flavors. Add parsley as garnish.

**Note from Nancy**

This is an elegant soup especially for summer luncheons. Adorn with edible flowers.

# Cold Gazpacho Soup    **Serves 10**

4 large ripe tomatoes, quartered

1 large sweet green pepper, quartered

1 large red pepper, quartered

1 medium zucchini, quartered

Three garlic cloves

1 cup or more of any or

all of the following mixed fresh herbs    Place first five ingredients into a blender.

(chives, parsley, basil, chervil and tarragon)    Blend into small pieces then transfer to a large container.

Place all herbs in a wooden chopping bowl and chop.

1/2 cup olive oil

5 tablespoons fresh lime juice

4 cups chilled beef stock

1 sweet or red onion, sliced

1 cucumber, quartered and seeded

1 1/2 teaspoon salt    Place these seven ingredients into a blender and blend

1/2 teaspoon paprika    into small pieces.

Mix all ingredients in a large container and refrigerate.

**Note from Nancy**

This is a wonderful summer recipe when vegetables are plentiful. Try adding pieces of shrimp,
feta cheese and sour cream. Make lots and keep in the fridge.

## Chicken or Turkey Roll-ups

**Serves 8**

2 chicken breasts, grilled, cut into strips
8 leaves of Boston lettuce or Bibb lettuce
Feta cheese
Roll-up dressing (in dressing section)

Place chicken in lettuce, sprinkle on cheese, add dressing and roll. This is also great with leftover turkey.

**Note from Nancy**

The variations are endless: tomato, red onion, avocado or alfalfa sprouts. Use your imagination.
For dressing recipe, look in the dressing section.

## Fruit Gazpacho

**Serves 8**

2 cups tomatoes, seeded and quartered
3 cups orange juice (freshly squeezed is best)
2 teaspoons sugar
Grated zest of 1 lime and 1 orange
2 cups cantaloupe, diced
2 cups honeydew melon, diced
1 mango, peeled and diced
1 apple, peeled and diced
1 cup fresh blueberries
1 cup seedless red grapes, diced
Strawberry or Kiwi slices garnish

Combine tomatoes, orange juice, sugar, orange and lime grated zest, cantaloupe, mango and melon in a large bowl. Process half the mixture in a food processor, blending until smooth. Process the other half. Combine in a large serving bowl with cover.

Stir in apple, blueberries, and grapes. Refrigerate for several hours.

Ladle the soup into bowls and garnish each serving with strawberries and/or kiwi slices.

**Note from Nancy**

Fruit gazpacho can be made from a combination of fruits such as berries and peaches. With these you may want to add a touch of cream and even a hint of your favorite liquor—such as quantro.

**Health note:** You may want to substitute stevia for the sugar. Two or three drops should be plenty.

## Nancy's Arugula Salad

**Serves 4**

1 pound of arugula
2 or 3 ounces of freshly grated Parmesan cheese
Fresh lemon juice to taste
Extra-virgin olive oil
1 pear, thinly sliced
Toasted pine nuts (optional)

Toss arugula and cheese together. Add fresh lemon juice and drizzle with olive oil. Place thinly sliced pear on top. Garnish with toasted pine nuts (optional). Serve immediately.

# Garden Coleslaw

**Serves 8**
Recipe by Merlene Jennings

THINLY SLICE

1/2 small cabbage

1/4 small purple cabbage

1/2 small red onion

1/2 green pepper

1 tart apple, unpeeled

1/2 cup shredded carrots

Juice of 1 lemon

Mix all ingredients together, and squeeze the juice of one lemon over the top.

## Dressing

2 tablespoons vinegar (white or red balsamic)

3 tablespoons olive oil

Sugar (or stevia) or honey to taste

Salt and pepper to taste

Mix all, and pour over coleslaw. Toss lightly. Refrigerate.

**Note from Nancy**

The lemon keeps the coleslaw fresh for days; therefore, this recipe can be doubled. This beautiful combination of healthy vegetables and fruit is surprisingly delicious. Also try it with soy sauce, olive oil and cashews or peanuts. Another great addition is cilantro and goat feta. What a wonderful, versatile recipe.

# Cold Potato Salad (Baby New)

**Serves 4**

10 to 15 small new potatoes

1 cup sour cream

Lots of fresh or dried dill

Sea salt and pepper

Cook potatoes until done but firm. Place potatoes in refrigerator until cold. Add sour cream, fresh dill, salt and pepper to taste. If fresh dill is not available, substitute dried dill.

**Note from Nancy**

This is a simple, elegant side dish for any season.

---

# Chilled Beet Salad (roasted)

**Serves 6**

3 pounds medium beets

3 tablespoons fresh lemon juice

1 1/2 tablespoons extra-virgin olive oil

3/4 teaspoon sweet paprika

1/2 teaspoon ground cumin

Preheat oven to 350°. Place beets on a cake pan and cover with foil. Bake until tender, about 1 1/2 hours. Cool, peel and cut into round slices, approximately 1/2 inch slices.

Combine the lemon juice, olive oil, paprika, cumin and salt to taste. Add beets and toss to coat. Add sea salt to taste.

Chill 20 minutes before serving.

# Feta Cheese & Green Bean Salad     **Serves 4**

1/2 pound green beans, halved
3 tablespoons red wine vinegar
2 garlic cloves, minced
1 1/2 small shallots, diced
1 teaspoon Dijon mustard or less to taste
2 tablespoons fresh oregano, chopped
1/2 teaspoon fresh thyme
1 large basil leaf
1/4 cup extra-virgin olive oil
Kosher salt and freshly ground pepper
1 pound grape tomatoes, halved
1/2 small red onion, chopped
1/4 pound feta cheese, crumbled (1 cup)

In a medium pot of boiling salted water, cook the green beans until just tender, about 4 minutes. Drain and rinse under cold water. Pat the beans dry.

In a blender, combine the red wine vinegar with the garlic cloves, shallots, mustard, oregano, thyme and basil, and puree until smooth. With the machine on, slowly add the olive oil. Season the vinaigrette with sea salt and pepper.

In a large bowl, combine the green beans, tomato halves, chopped onion and crumbled feta cheese. Toss with the vinaigrette and serve the salad immediately.

# Basic Tuna Salad     **Serving for 8**

2 (12 ounce) cans Albacore tuna in water, drained
4 green onions, chopped (red onion optional)
Mayonnaise to taste

Mix ingredients and serve.

**Variations:** Include green olives, boiled eggs, dill relish, white onion or capers.

# Nancy's Avocado and Black Bean Salad

**Serves 8**

Juice of 1/2 fresh lime

2 tablespoons extra-virgin olive oil

1 (15 ounce) can organic black beans, rinsed and drained

1/2 green pepper, chopped

1/2 red onion, chopped

Chop fresh garlic to taste

Salt, pepper and red pepper flakes

Handful of fresh cilantro, snipped

4 avocados (save the shells), sliced lengthwise

Scoop out avocado with spoon, chop

Mix lime juice and olive oil, whisk together. Stir in beans, peppers, onion, garlic, salt, pepper and red pepper flakes if desired. Stir in cilantro. Add avocados. Place mixture in shells. Top with sour cream.

# Garbanzo Bean Salad with Fresh Cilantro

**Serves 10**

4 (15 ounce) cans of garbanzo beans

1 (16 ounce) jar of chunky tomato salsa, medium or hot

1/2 medium red onion, chopped

2 to 4 fresh garlic cloves, chopped

Generous handful fresh cilantro, chopped

1 cup real mayonnaise

Drain beans and combine the remaining ingredients. Refrigerate.

I always insist on fresh cilantro. You can use more or less depending on taste. Green, red or white onions are just as good in this recipe.

**Note from Nancy**

Actress Jane Seymour, a friend and fellow artist, while staying in my home requested this recipe. When making this recipe, I resort to using canned products, but I always insist on using organic!

## Bean and Wild Rice Salad  Serves 10

3 cups cooked real wild rice, chilled
1 (15 ounce) can red beans, rinsed and drained
1 (15 ounce) can black beans, rinsed and drained
1 (10 ounce) package frozen peas, thawed
1 cup celery, chopped
1 medium red onion, chopped
2 (4 ounce) cans diced chili peppers, drained
1/2 cup cilantro, snipped
Feta Cheese

In large covered container combine the above ingredients and mix well. Sprinkle with feta cheese before serving.

## Garlic Dressing

COMBINE
1/3 cup white wine vinegar
1/4 cup olive oil
2 tablespoons cold water
3/4 teaspoon salt
1/2 teaspoon garlic powder
(or 3 garlic cloves, minced)

Transfer to a jar with a lid and shake or mix well.
Add dressing to salad (more or less to taste).

# Wild Rice and Vegetable Salad    **Serves 4**

2 cups chicken broth (organic)

1 cup wild rice

1 small bunch broccoli, cut into florets

4 ounces fresh green beans, cut into pieces

6 fresh asparagus spears, cut into pieces

2 carrots, chopped

1 tomato, chopped

1/2 cup blue cheese, crumbled

1/4 cup olive oil

2 tablespoons white wine vinegar

Salt and pepper to taste

Bring chicken broth to a boil in heavy medium saucepan. Stir in rice, reduce heat, cover and simmer until rice is tender, about I hour. Meanwhile, cook broccoli, green beans, asparagus and carrots in pot of boiling water until crisp-tender, about 5 minutes. Drain rice. Rinse vegetables under cold water.

Transfer rice to casserole dish. Place vegetables atop rice and sprinkle with tomato and cheese. Mix olive oil and vinegar. Drizzle mixture over salad and toss thoroughly. Season with salt and pepper.

---

# Pea Salad    **Serves 6**

2 (10 ounce) packages frozen peas

3 green onions, chopped

1 1/2 cups celery, chopped

12 green olives, chopped and pitted

1 medium carrot, chopped

1 small red bell pepper, chopped

1/4 cup mayonnaise

1 1/2 teaspoon soy sauce

Combine all ingredients and toss until well coated. Refrigerate. Serve with fresh fish of your choice.

**Optional:** Add a handful of fresh cilantro.

# Stuffed Tomatoes

**Serves 4**

4 plum tomatoes, halved lengthwise

3 tablespoons Parmesan cheese, freshly grated

2 garlic cloves, minced

3 to 4 tablespoons of fresh basil, chopped

3 ounces mozzarella cheese

Salt and pepper

Preheat oven to 400°. Scoop out inside of each tomato and chop the pulp. Combine the pulp, Parmesan, garlic, basil, mozzarella, and salt and pepper to taste.

**Some variations:**

Goat feta, pine nuts, parsley or tarragon

Place tomatoes, cut side up, on baking sheet. Spoon in tomato mixture and bake until cheese is melted and lightly browned, about 10 minutes. Serve warm.

# Tomato Pie with Bacon, Cheese & Basil

**Serves 6**

1 (9 inch) deep-dish pie shell, baked and cooled

6 or 7 medium red tomatoes, cut into chunks

4 tablespoons fresh basil, chopped

3 tablespoons fresh chives, chopped

12 slices of bacon, fried and crumbled

Salt and pepper

1 cup real mayonnaise

1 cup grated cheddar cheese (reserve 1/2 cup cheese for top)

Preheat oven to 350°. Fill pie shell with tomatoes, basil, chives and bacon. Salt and pepper to taste. Mix mayonnaise and cheese and spread evenly over top of tomato mixture. Bake for 30 minutes or until lightly browned.

**Note from Nancy**

Remember this when ripe tomatoes are plentiful.

*Dressings*

# Make your own!

Dressings are very important, and I always encourage friends to make their own. Most bottled dressings contain harmful preservatives, colorings and unnecessary chemicals.

## Real Mayonnaise

1 egg and 1 egg yoke
1 capful of white wine vinegar
3 teaspoons fresh lemon juice
1/2 teaspoon Dijon mustard
2 dashes of Worcestershire sauce
Salt and pepper to taste
1 cup olive oil

Blend all ingredients in blender. Add 1 cup of olive oil and blend until smooth.

**Note from Nancy**

Please help yourself to some creative taste ideas, such as adding garlic powder, soy sauce, and fresh herbs (chives, fresh dill, basil or parsley).

## Nancy's Everyday Dressing

One-half vinegar and one-half olive oil, depending on the amount of dressing needed. Add a small drop or two of Grey Poupon mustard and honey to taste. Mix well.

— N

# Creamy Dressing

1/2 cup chilled heavy whipping cream

1/4 cup buttermilk

1/4 cup mayonnaise

2 tablespoons blanched almonds, chopped finely

2 1/2 tablespoons lemon juice

12 large fresh basil leaves, chopped

Salt and pepper to taste

Mix all ingredients in bowl and blend until smooth.
Cover and refrigerate adding fresh basil just before serving.

**Note from Nancy**

Try this dressing on veggies such as asparagus, green beans and, of course,
your favorite salad. This dressing can be prepared one day ahead.

# Basil Salad Dressing

3 tablespoons basil oil

1 teaspoon honey

1 teaspoon garlic, minced

1 teaspoon prepared mustard (organic if possible)

1 tablespoon apple cider vinegar

Salt and pepper

Puree all ingredients in a blender.

**Note from Nancy**

Serve over fresh spinach, arugula or a mixture of salad greens. This is a versatile dressing without MSGs,
trans-fatty acids or preservatives.

# Poppy Seed Dressing

Recipe by Jerome Noël

6 tablespoons sour cream
6 tablespoons mayonnaise
3 tablespoons of honey
1 tablespoon red wine vinegar
4 tablespoons poppy seeds

Mix all the ingredients together. Serve over iceburg lettuce, spinach or mixed greens with red onions, apples and grated white cheddar cheese.

# Blue Cheese Dressing

6 ounces sherry vinegar
5 garlic cloves, finely chopped
16 ounces blue cheese
16 ounces sour cream
16 ounces mayonnaise
2 teaspoons parsley, chopped
1 tablespoon Worcestershire sauce
Black pepper to taste

Simmer vinegar, garlic and 1/4 of blue cheese in saucepan over low heat. Cool. Fold in the rest of the ingredients. Mix well. Refrigerate until ready to use.

Edible Flowers

A good rule of thumb is, if you cannot positively identify a flower as edible, don't eat it. Do not eat flowers picked from the roadside or from a florist, as these may have been sprayed with chemicals.

Eat only the flowers, remove the pistils and stamens. If you have allergies, please use caution.

The most common and safest edible flowers are nasturtium, pansy, violet, Johnny-jump-up, calendula, chive and sage. These flowers can be easily grown without the use of pesticides and chemicals.

Some of the flowers of herbs, vegetables and fruits that are commonly eaten include: basil, banana, broccoli, chervil, cilantro, dandelions, daylilies, dill, fennel, garlic, lemon verbena, mint, oregano, peach and pear blossoms, rosemary, and thyme.

Edible flowers have become common as garnishes in restaurants. Use them at home, on soups and salads and they will not only add color, but also flavor.

Try freezing the petals in ice cube trays filled with water, and then add them to your favorite iced tea or lemonade. Experience some magic.

# Cat in the Kitchen

## eggs, cheese & cream

Eggs are often referred to as the perfect food. Remember that all dairy is not created equal. We always recommend organic. Here we have hatched some of my favorite combination recipes using eggs, cheese and cream.

## Nancy's Deviled Eggs

**Serves 10**

12 eggs, boiled and peeled

3 tablespoons mayonnaise

1 tablespoon red wine vinegar, apple cider vinegar, or balsamic vinegar

1 teaspoon Dijon mustard

2 heaping tablespoons dill relish

Slice eggs lengthwise and remove yokes. Mix yokes with remaining ingredients until smooth. Place mixture into eggs. Salt and pepper if needed.

## Basic Quiche  Serves 6

1 (9 inch) pastry crust

5 eggs

1 cup whipping cream

1/4 cup milk

1/2 teaspoon dry mustard

Salt and pepper to taste

1 1/2 cup cheese (your choice)

Bake pastry crust at 425° for 10 to 15 minutes or until lightly brown.

Beat eggs. Add cream, milk and seasonings. Layer 1/2 of cheese on bottom of crust. Add egg mixture, then the other half of the cheese on top. Reduce temperature to 350° and bake until brown on top or sharp knife comes out clean.

**Note from Nancy**

This quiche can be made with ham, bacon, broccoli, asparagus, onions, spinach and any other ingredients that are special for you.

# Alexander's Spinach and Feta Quiche

**Serves 6**

3 cloves garlic

3 tablespoons fresh spinach

2 large eggs

1 egg yolk

8 ounces feta cheese, divided

1 2/3 cup whipping cream

1 unbaked pie crust

15 cherry tomatoes, sliced into halves and mixed with 1 tablespoon olive oil

Preheat oven to 350°. Using a mortar and pestle, make a paste out of the garlic cloves, small amount of oil and a pinch of salt.

Wash and stem the spinach and steam quickly. Pour into a large colander and press out all of the water (this is very important).

Beat the eggs and the yolk. Stir in the garlic paste and feta. Blend in the cream. Add salt and pepper to taste.

Layer the spinach into the piecrust and pour the egg mixture over it. Spread the tomatoes on top. Sprinkle with other half of feta cheese. Bake for 25 to 30 minutes or until cheese is brown on top.

**Note from Nancy**

This recipe came from my son Alexander. It is now a regular delight around the house, especially when we have company.

## Shrimp Quiche

**Serves 6**

2 cups cooked shrimp, cut into medium-size pieces
(refrigerate until needed)

1 (9 inch) pie shell
5 eggs
1 cup whipping cream
1/4 cup milk
1 teaspoon garlic, finely chopped (more if you like the taste)
1 1/2 cup goat cheddar cheese, shredded and divided
Salt and pepper to taste
1/2 lemon squeezed in a bowl (set aside)

Bake pie shell at 425° for 15 to 20 minutes until light brown.

Beat eggs, add cream, milk and seasonings. Layer 1/2 of the cheese on the bottom of the crust. Add egg mixture, shrimp with lemon and the other half of the cheese on top. Reduce heat to 350° and bake 30 to 45 minutes or until brown on top or sharp knife comes out clean.

**Note from Nancy**

The goat cheddar gives this quiche a distinctive flavor all its own. Substitute the cheese of your choice.

---

## Seafood Salad

**Serves 6**

2 cups fresh cooked crab or cooked shrimp
2 to 3 eggs, boiled and chopped
2 green onions, finely chopped
2 to 3 tablespoons mayonnaise
1 fresh lemon
2 tablespoons fresh dill
Salt and pepper

Chop crab and/or shrimp into medium-size pieces. Add eggs, green onions, mayonnaise and the juice of 1/2 lemon. Add fresh dill, salt and pepper. Depending upon your taste, squeeze in the remaining lemon juice. Refrigerate and serve cold.

Dill weed can be substituted for fresh dill.

*Halloumi Cheese— you'll like it!*

This cheese is becoming more readily available in the U.S. When traveling to Africa, I always have a salad with fried or grilled Halloumi cheese.

### Fry it

1 (8 ounce) package of Halloumi Cheese

Slice into 8 slices and place in a skillet, no butter or oil necessary; however, I use a tiny amount of butter. The cheese will cook in its own brine. Sauté over medium heat on both sides until golden brown.

One of Nancy's favorite salads is arugula, red onions, fresh chopped tomatoes, fresh parsley, basil, balsamic vinegar and garlic with squeezed lime, fresh oregano and drizzled olive oil. Top with fried Halloumi Cheese. Nancy also suggests sliced tomatoes, a generous handful of chopped parsley and basil. Top with slices of grilled Halloumi and drizzle with red balsamic vinegar.

### Grill it

Thread cubes of Halloumi cheese onto skewers with mushrooms, onions and peppers. Grill over low to medium heat until cheese is golden brown, turning frequently. Season with garlic salt or dried oregano, be creative.

### Grate it

Try grated Halloumi cheese over pizza, pasta or in soup. Add it to an omelet for a special treat. This cheese adds wonderful Mediterranean flavor to any meal.

# Fall Harvest
## hot soups, breads & stuffing

Fall brings with it a whole variety of feel-good foods that we often overlook. Don't put them on the back burner. Here are some healthy, hearty recipes for the hearth and heart.

## Banana Nut Bread    **Makes 3 small loaves**

1 stick of butter, softened
1 cup of sugar
2 eggs
1 cup very ripe bananas
1 1/4 cups flour
3/4 teaspoon soda
1/2 teaspoon salt
1/8 teaspoon baking powder
1 cup of pecans or walnuts

Cream butter and sugar until fluffy. Add eggs one at a time. Beat well. Stir-in the bananas (smashed).

Sift dry ingredients together. Add to banana mixture. Add nuts and mix well.

Pour into small greased pans. Bake at 350° approximately 30 to 35 minutes.

**Note from Nancy**
This is an all-time favorite at my house. You can add more bananas if you like. This bread freezes well.

# Zucchini Bread

3 medium-size zucchinis, grated and well drained,
approximately 2 cups

3 eggs

1 cup coconut oil (vegetable oil is optional)

1 1/2 cups sugar

2 teaspoons vanilla

2 cups of all-purpose flour

1/4 teaspoon baking powder

2 teaspoons baking soda

3 teaspoons ground cinnamon

1 teaspoon salt

1 1/2 cups pecans and/or walnuts, chopped

Beat eggs lightly in a large bowl. Stir in oil, sugar,
zucchini and vanilla.

Sift all dry ingredients together onto wax paper. Stir into
egg mixture. Stir-in nuts. Spoon batter into a well-greased
8 x 5 x 3-inch loaf pan.

Bake at 375° for 1 hour or until center springs back when
pressed with fingertip. Cool in pan for 10 minutes. Remove
from pan and cool completely.

# Bread Pudding with Caramel Sauce

**Serves 5**
Recipe by Keltie Domina

24 ounces of bread (preferably plain), cubed and left overnight

1 pound sugar

1/2 gallon heavy whipping cream

2 tablespoons vanilla

10 eggs

Place bread cubes in casserole dish and sprinkle with cinnamon.

Add sugar, heavy cream and vanilla to large sauce pan. Bring to a boil, stirring constantly. Remove from heat.

Add the 10 eggs to mixing bowl and whisk together about 30 seconds.

Slowly add the eggs in with the custard, constantly stirring the mixture. Pour custard over bread and allow to stand about 15 minutes.

Place in preheated oven 350°. Cover and bake for 20 minutes. Remove cover and continue baking for an additional 10 to 15 minutes or until golden brown.

# Caramel Sauce

16 ounces brown sugar

1 pint heavy whipping cream

3/4 cup melted butter

Add brown sugar, heavy cream and butter to medium sauce pan and bring to a boil, stirring constantly. Allow to cool.

Once cooled slightly, ladle sauce over each serving of bread pudding.

# Gingery Carrot Soup

**Serves 8**
Recipe by Sheila Lindsay

3 tablespoons butter or olive oil
4 cups carrots, chopped
2 cups onions or leeks, chopped
1 cup potatoes, chopped
1 tablespoon fresh gingerroot, grated
2 1/2 cups organic chicken broth
2 cups whipping cream

In large heavy saucepan, melt butter over medium low heat. Cook carrots, leeks, potatoes, and gingerroot, stirring until vegetables are softened. Add your favorite seasonings and stock. Bring to boil, reduce heat, cover and simmer for 20 minutes or until vegetables are very tender. Blend in food processor or blender until smooth.

When ready to serve, add cream.

**Note from Nancy**

Soup, without cream, can be frozen for up to 4 months, or it will keep in an airtight container in refrigerator for up to 2 weeks.

# Simple Tomato Soup

**Serves 8**

Garlic and white onion, chopped
Butter
2 or 3 large tomatoes, chopped
White wine
Dash of hot sauce or cayenne pepper

Sauté garlic and onion in butter until tender. Add chopped tomatoes and white wine to cover tomatoes. Cook only until warm, gently stirring.

May be served with croutons, your favorite cheese or sour cream. Add hot sauce to taste.

# *Broccoli Soup*

2 medium crowns of broccoli (save the stalks)
1 medium white onion
1 large can organic chicken broth
Small amount of butter and olive oil
Cumin, salt and pepper to taste
Cream

Divide the broccoli into florets and stalks. Chop the stalks into 1/2 slices and sauté with chopped onion in butter and olive oil, until stalks are tender, adding water as necessary to prevent sticking.

Continue to simmer about 20 minutes. Blend until smooth, using an electric, handheld wand mixer. Add chicken broth, and on low heat, simmer for approximately 1 hour.
Steam the florets, chop and add to mixture of chicken broth and stalks. Continue to simmer until ready to serve. Add cream, cumin, salt and pepper to taste. Right before serving, add some cream to each bowl.

**Tip:** This soup can be simmered in a slow cooker.

**Note from Nancy**

A healthy and easy soup which also can be made with asparagus.

# Healthy Chicken Soup

**Serves 8 to 10**

6 large chicken breasts, cooked and cubed

1 cup carrots (cook in chicken broth
for approximately 20 minutes)

CHOP AND SAUTÉ THE
FOLLOWING UNTIL TENDER

1 small onion

1/2 green pepper

1/2 red pepper

1/2 orange pepper

5 stalks celery

Olive Oil

2 bay leaves

Generous amount of cumin

Salt and pepper to taste

**Optional:** Fresh green beans, zucchini, mushrooms,
potatoes, tomatoes and jalapenos are all optional

Cook carrots in chicken broth for approximately 20 minutes. Chop onion, peppers, and celery, or your choice of vegetables. Sauté in olive oil and bay leaves until tender.

Place all of the ingredients into a slow cooker. Add cumin, salt and pepper to taste. Simmer for approximately 2 hours in a slow cooker.

Add about 1 tablespoon sour cream to each bowl right before serving.

**Tip:** Kitchen scissors are great for cubing chicken.

**Note from Nancy**

Try adding some hot sauce for a little zip, or combine with wild rice.
This is a staple in our house, especially in the winter!

# Rosie's Simply Divine Thanksgiving Dressing

1 loaf of bread, toasted
1 large white onion, chopped
1 stick of butter

Grind toasted bread in food processor or blender. Melt butter in large skillet and sauté onion until tender. Add breadcrumbs and toss gently, until breadcrumbs are thoroughly mixed with butter. Remove from heat and sprinkle with salt and pepper to taste. Top with turkey gravy and serve.

**Note from Nancy**

This Danish recipe was handed down to me by Rosie, my grandmother's cook. This is absolutely the only Thanksgiving dressing I use.

# Do-ahead Mashed Potatoes

**Serves 10 to 12**

5 pounds potatoes, peeled and quartered

6 ounces cream cheese

1 cup sour cream

2 egg whites

2 teaspoons onion or garlic powder

1 teaspoon salt

1/4 teaspoon white or black pepper

1 tablespoon butter

Cook potatoes in boiling water until tender. Drain. Mash until smooth with mixer.

Add cream cheese, sour cream, egg whites, onion powder, salt and pepper. Mix well and add to potatoes.

Cool, cover and store in refrigerator. May be used anytime within 2 weeks.

To use, place desired amount in greased casserole, dot with butter. Bake 350° until heated, about 30 to 40 minutes.

**Note from Nancy**

Once you make these you'll never go back to making mashed potatoes the day of your dinner.

## Black Bean Chili

**Serves 8**

2 pounds black dried beans

1 medium onion

1 green pepper

1 red pepper

1 quart tomatoes

Salt, pepper and cumin to taste

Fresh oregano, minced

Sour cream

Cook beans until almost soft. Sauté onion and green and red pepper in butter until tender.

Transfer beans to slow cooker. Add the sautéed ingredients and tomatoes. Add a generous amount of salt, pepper and cumin to taste.

Cook for one hour on low to medium heat, then add a handful of fresh minced oregano. Continue cooking for another hour.

Top with sour cream and serve.

**Note from Nancy**

This is a wonderfully hearty, vegetarian, protein-packed, meal-in-one. A favorite of both my sons.

# Apple Information

Nutritional Information: One medium apple contains about 80 calories; 4 grams of fiber; about 150 milligrams of potassium and 8 milligrams of vitamin C; no sodium; no cholesterol; and 22 grams carbohydrates.

When shopping for apples, look for smooth skin and good color. Green apples are usually more tart than red. Apples will continue to ripen at room temperature, so unless you are going to eat them immediately, refrigerate them in a plastic bag that contains a moistened paper towel.

**Best Uses:**
• Jonathan apples are good for eating, baking whole and cider.
• Granny Smith, Winesap, Jonathan and Paula Red are good for pies.
• Fuji, Gala, Jonathan, Red Delicious and Winesap are great eating apples.
• Golden Delicious can be used in making dumplings.
• Fuji and Paula Red's are good for applesauce.

My grandmother use to say, "An apple a day keeps the doctor away," That's something to think about.

---

# Apple Dumplings

**Serves 6**
Recipe by Louise Malachowski

2 (9 inch) pie crusts
6 apples, medium in size
Cinnamon dots (red hots)
Butter
2 cups light brown sugar
1 cup water
Sour cream

Peel and core apples. I suggest using a baking apple. Fill each apple with red hots and top with a teaspoon of butter.

Divide the two pie crusts into a total of 6 individual pieces of pastry. Place an apple on each piece. Bring up the corners of the pastry and seal the seam with a small amount of water. Place apples in an ungreased baking dish.

In a small saucepan, bring sugar and water to a boil. Pour mixture of sugar and water over the apples. Bake at 425° for approximately 30 minutes, basting every 10 minutes.

Serve warm with sour cream. Add a small amount of powdered sugar, if desired.

# Cooking Pumpkins

Smaller pumpkins are best for cooking. Wash pumpkin and scrub with brush to remove dirt. Cut the pumpkin in half, crosswise, with a large knife and remove the seeds with your hands. If smaller hands are available, by all means use them. This is one job they will love. Save the seeds for later.

Place the pumpkin, shell side up, in a 9 x 13 baking pan. Bake at 325° until tender, about 1 hour. Scrape the pulp from the shell and mash to a fine consistency. Pumpkin can be frozen and used for pies, soups, muffins and breads.

---

# Baked Pumpkin Seeds

The seeds you saved can now be baked and eaten for a healthy snack.

Rinse and pat dry the seeds. In a small bowl combine 1 tablespoon of olive oil and sprinkle with salt. Add seeds and toss to coat. Place on a cookie sheet, in one layer, and bake at 325° for 30 minutes, stirring occasionally. Reduce heat to 250° and bake 1 hour. Let cool, and eat the fruits of your labor.

# Harmony
## Fish, Chicken, pork and beef

It is my belief that the care and feeding of the livestock we consume can have a direct effect on our lives. I personally eat very little meat however, when I do, I try to be sure it's organic and 100% grassfed! Meat, poultry and fish should be raised free to enjoy life and honored as a gift to us.

---

## Herb-broiled Shrimp

**Serves 6**

20 to 30 shrimp
6 garlic cloves
1 bunch cilantro
2 tablespoons olive oil
8 tablespoons butter

Place the rack of the broiler about 8 inches from the top.

Rinse the cilantro, cut the stems off, and shake off remaining water. Put cilantro and garlic in food processor. Add the olive oil, and process until mixed.

Melt butter in microwave. Place shrimp in baking dish, large enough for all the shrimp. Season with salt and pepper to taste. Spread the cilantro mixture and melted butter over shrimp.

Broil 10 to 12 minutes until shrimp are golden brown.

# Lime Butter and Salmon

**Serves 4**

4 (9 ounce) salmon fillets
1 stick butter, melted
1/4 cup lime juice
1 tablespoon coarse black pepper (if desired)

Lime wedges for garnish

Combine butter, lime juice and pepper. Arrange salmon in glass baking dish. Pour mixture over salmon. Let marinate for several hours to enhance the flavor. Cook salmon over medium heat on grill until just opaque, continually brushing with lime butter. Transfer to warmed plates, and garnish with lime wedges.

# Smoked Salmon Patties

**Serves 8**

2 pounds smoked salmon
4 slices bread, toasted and broken into pieces
2 eggs
2 tablespoons fresh lemon juice
A handful fresh dill, chopped

**Optional:**
Onion powder or garlic powder to taste

Place all ingredients in food processor and blend until smooth and mixed well. Form into patties. Fry in small amount of olive oil and butter over medium heat until brown on both sides.

This recipe is great for leftover salmon. Simply adjust the ingredients.

If the mixture is too dry, try adding some milk to moisten before frying.

Spice it up with hot sauce or wasabi mayonnaise before serving.

# Pasta with Mushrooms, Sour Cream and Parmesan Cheese

**Serves 6**

8 ounces pasta (your choice)
1/2 cup sour cream
1/2 cup Parmesan cheese, grated
8 ounces mushrooms (your choice)
Minced garlic to taste
Small amount of butter and olive oil

Sauté mushrooms and garlic in butter and olive oil.

Cook pasta according to directions on package, rinse in warm water and drain.

While pasta is still hot, add sour cream and Parmesan cheese, then mix with mushrooms and garlic. Serve hot.

# Angel Hair Pasta with Shrimp

**Serves 4**

1 package of angel hair pasta (enough for 4 people)
20 cooked shrimp, tails removed
20 cherry tomatoes
2 or 3 garlic cloves, chopped
Olive oil and butter
Freshly grated Parmesan cheese

Cook pasta according to the directions on package.

Sauté shrimp, tomatoes and garlic in a small amount of olive oil and butter, until the skins of the tomatoes begin to crack.

Season with salt and pepper, sprinkle with Parmesan cheese, and serve over pasta.

# Poaching Fish or Chicken

Poaching is simply cooking fish or chicken in wine, vegetable broth or other liquid of choice.

In a saucepan with lid, pour in wine (Chardonnay or Pinot Gregio), enough to barely cover fish. Place vegetables on top. Tomatoes, onions, mushrooms, spinach, garlic, peppers and fresh herbs or any vegetables or herbs of your choice are wonderful additions to place on top of the fish.

Heat wine in saucepan to a simmer, place lid on saucepan, and cook until fish flakes (about 20 minutes). Season with your favorite spices and a squeeze of fresh lemon. Serve warm.

Poaching produces little odor, and the clean up is easy.

**Tip:** Store liquid in refrigerator and use again.

Another option is to sauté fish or chicken in butter/ olive oil (few minutes on each side until top is golden brown). Follow the above directions for poaching.

# Chicken Salad for Sandwiches　**Serves 6**

2 cups of chicken, cooked and cubed
1 1/2 cups celery, chopped
3/4 cup to 1 cup real mayonnaise
(more or less; also, see recipe for homemade mayo)

Combine ingredients. Serve cold.

**Note from Nancy**

I always receive compliments on this simple chicken salad.

# Barb Hasbrook's Chicken Salad

Serves 8 to 10

4 chicken breasts, cooked and cubed

1 bunch scallions or green onions, chopped

4 stalks celery, chopped

1 cup sugar snap peas, sliced

1 cup dried cranberries

1 1/2 cups pecans, toasted

1 cup real mayonnaise

3/4 cup basil leaves, chopped

1 tablespoon butter

2 tablespoons olive oil

Basil oil, salt and pepper to taste

Sauté sugar snap peas in butter until they turn bright green, then set aside. Mix all ingredients together with mayonnaise and olive oil. Drizzle with basil oil if desired.

**Note from Nancy**

My friend Barb Hasbrook is famous for many things. Her chicken salad is one of them. This is great for entertaining and a meal-in-one for the family. Double this recipe. It will be consumed rapidly. Remember, creative cooking is adding more or less to your taste. (No bread or crackers required with this dish.)

---

# Greek Chicken Salad

Serves 8

Recipe by Flo Brill

3 cup cooked chicken, cubed

2 medium cucumbers, peeled, seeded and chopped

1 1/4 cup feta cheese, crumbled

2/3 cup ripe black olives, sliced

1/4 cup parsley, snipped

1 cup mayonnaise

3 cloves garlic, chopped

1 teaspoon fresh or dried oregano

1/2 cup plain yogurt

Combine first 5 ingredients and set aside. Mix all other ingredients in small bowl. Add to chicken mixture and toss to coat. Cover and refrigerate. Serve on a bed of Bibb lettuce.

# Chicken and Sun-dried Tomatoes

**Serves 6**
Recipe by Demetra Turner

4 chicken breasts, cut into cubes

2 (4 ounce) packages sun-dried tomatoes

1 small onion, chopped

2 garlic cloves, minced

Handful of fresh basil, chopped

1 to 2 cups half and half

3 tablespoons olive oil

Salt and pepper to taste

Sauté chicken in olive oil over medium heat until brown and tender. Add onion and sauté for one minute. Then add garlic and sauté for four minutes. Add tomatoes, basil, salt and pepper. Add half and half and simmer but do not boil.

**Note from Nancy**

This recipe is very versatile. You can add toasted pine nuts, feta, goat or regular cheese. This recipe can be served over wild rice or pasta. It can also be saved and added to an omelet or a spinach salad.

# Fennel Chicken with Lime & Ginger

**Serves 8**

4 boneless chicken breasts, cooked and cubed

2 tablespoons fennel seed

Juice of 2 limes, squeezed (save lime peels)

4 tablespoons olive oil, divided

1/4 teaspoon red pepper flakes

2 to 4 plums and/or nectarines, thinly sliced

2 green onions, chopped

2 tablespoons fresh ginger, grated

3 cups packed spinach leaves or romaine lettuce

Heat skillet over medium heat. Toast fennel seeds, shaking until fragrant (approximately 2 minutes). Combine 1 tablespoon olive oil, 1 tablespoon lime juice, 1/2 teaspoon salt and fennel seeds in shallow bowl. Add chicken to this mixture and marinate in refrigerator while preparing the rest of the recipe.

**Dressing:**

Whisk remaining 3 tablespoons olive oil, 1 tablespoon lime juice, salt and pepper to taste, pepper flakes, and a small amount of shaved lime peel in bowl.

**Fruit Mixture:**

In separate bowl, toss fruit, green onions and remaining 2 tablespoons of lime juice and 2 tablespoons of grated fresh ginger.

Slice marinated chicken into 1/2"-wide strips and sauté until tender (approximately 4 to 5 minutes on each side). Toss greens with lime dressing and place on a platter. Top with chicken and spoon on fruit. Garnish with lime.

**Note**: Use plums or nectarines, whichever you prefer. Serve over spinach or Romaine lettuce, or both.

**Optional:** Add 1 or 2 cups of watercress. For added flavor, garnish with the zest of lime peel. I always use extra virgin olive oil.

**Note from Nancy**

World-class race driver Emerson Fitapaldi came to dinner one evening in May, right before the Indy 500. Knowing he is health-conscience and that he routinely dines on some of the world's best foods, I served this favorite all-in-one light meal. God forbid that I would have served something that may have interfered with the outcome of the race. All went well. He loved my chicken salad, insisted on having the recipe, and won the race that year.

# Fried Chicken    **Serves 6**

6 boneless chicken breasts

4 eggs

2 cups of milk or buttermilk

Slice chicken breasts in quarters. Beat the eggs, add the milk, and marinate chicken overnight in the refrigerator.

Dredge the marinated chicken in flour mixed with salt, pepper and garlic powder. Heat olive oil in heavy skillet. Fry chicken, turning repeatedly until golden brown and tender.

**Optional:** Add 1/2 stick of butter to the olive oil.

# Grilled Chicken with Lemon and Sage    **Serves 8**

4 large boneless chicken breasts, cut into halves

3/4 cup fresh lemon juice

6 tablespoons extra-virgin olive oil

1/4 cup fresh sage, chopped

(or use 1 tablespoon dried sage)

2 teaspoons honey

Dash of hot pepper sauce

(or more if you prefer)

Mix all the ingredients and coat both sides of chicken. Marinate for about 1 hour. Grill over medium-high heat, brushing frequently with marinade. Cook until chicken is no longer pink and is browned evenly.

**Note from Nancy**

Always make your own marinades. They're so easy. Bottled marinades are usually full of MSGs and a variety of unnecessary and unhealthy chemicals.

# Michael's Baked Chicken with Sherry

**Serves 8**
This recipe came from my son Michael

6 boneless chicken breasts
2 tablespoons garlic salt
2 tablespoons paprika
6 tablespoons butter
1/2 cup real lemon juice
1 cup sour cream
1/4 cup cooking sherry wine
1/2 pound mushrooms, sliced

Place chicken in glass baking dish. Melt butter and add paprika, garlic salt and lemon juice. Pour over chicken. Bake at 350° for 1 hour.

Combine sour cream and sherry. Remove chicken from oven and add the mixture and the mushrooms on top of chicken. Bake for an additional 15 minutes.

Serve with rice, salad or fresh vegetables.

# Glazed Pork with Honey and Garlic

**Serves 8**

1 (4 pound) center-cut boneless pork loin roast
1 cup honey (more if desired)
5 garlic cloves, minced
3 teaspoons fresh rosemary, minced (optional)

Place pork on roasting rack in pan. Mix honey, minced garlic and rosemary (optional) in a small mixing bowl. Coat roast with mixture. Season with salt and pepper.

Bake 325° for approximately 2 hours, basting with honey and garlic mixture. Remove and let sit for 10 minutes before carving.

# *Beef Stew*  **Serves 4 to 6**

3 pounds boneless beef roast, cut into 1 1/2 inch pieces

3 medium carrots, sliced

3 stalks celery, cut into 1/2 inch pieces

2 medium onions, sliced into 1/2 inch pieces

2 or 3 large potatoes, cut into 1/2 inch pieces

2 tablespoons butter

**Broth**

2 tablespoons red currant jelly (optional)

2 cups dry red wine

2 cups beef stock or broth

2 sprigs of thyme

2 garlic cloves, minced

1 bay leaf

In large heavy pot, heat 2 tablespoons of olive oil until shimmering. Dredge the beef in flour, season with salt and pepper. Brown meat on both sides, transfer the meat to a bowl.

Using the same pot, melt the butter. Add carrots, celery, onions and potatoes and cook over medium to low heat, stirring occasionally, until onion is caramelized. Add jelly (optional) and wine and bring to a boil, stirring until well mixed.

Add beef, thyme, garlic and bay leaf and simmer over low heat until meat is tender. Remove beef and vegetables. Boil the sauce over high heat until reduced to 2 cups, about 10 minutes. Return meat and vegetables to sauce. Season with salt and pepper. Remove thyme and bay leaf.

# Pot Roast Italian Style

**Serves 8 to 10**

1 (4 to 5 pounds) sirloin roast

2 teaspoons salt and pepper

2 tablespoons olive oil

2 cloves garlic, minced

1 tablespoon of fresh basil, chopped

1 whole onion, with 2 cloves inserted (whole)

3 carrots, sliced

1 (15 ounce) can tomato puree

1/2 cup red wine

1 tablespoon of fresh parsley, chopped

Rub roast with 2 teaspoons of salt and pepper. In large pot, brown roast in 2 tablespoons of olive oil. Add 2 minced garlic cloves and basil.

Add onion, carrots, tomato puree and 1/2 cup red wine. Cover and bring to a boil. Then simmer 2 to 3 hours or until meat is tender. Discard onion, remove roast and slice.

Garnish with parsley and serve.

# Slow-baked Baby Back Ribs

**Serves 4 to 6**

2 or 3 slabs of ribs
5 cloves garlic, chopped
Rice vinegar
Organic soy sauce
Honey

Rub ribs with honey until lightly covered.

Place ribs on heavy-duty foil in a shallow baking pan. Cover ribs completely with organic soy sauce, 5 cloves of chopped garlic and rice vinegar. Let marinate over night if possible. Seal the foil around the edges and the top, then bake at 325° for approximately 3 hours.

Peppers and onions can be added on top of ribs during cooking if desired.

# The French Finale

*only the best desserts*

I love sweets—but not too sweet. Here is a variety of versatile desserts, some elegant and some down to earth. To accompany these desserts, remember that edible flowers make a fabulous finale. Don't miss our section on edible flowers.

⊶⊷

## A quick and easy dessert, snack or appetizer

I pick strawberries from the garden, leaving the little green leaves on the top. Then I set out a small bowl of sour cream and a small bowl of loose, light brown sugar.

First dip the strawberry in the sour cream, then into the brown sugar, and into your mouth. Delicious.

# Fruit Dip

1 jar of marshmallow cream

1 package of cream cheese

Orange extract flavoring and liquid ginger to taste

Combine all ingredients until smooth. Serve with the fruit of your choice.

This is a great dip for strawberries, apples, melons, bananas and kiwis.

---

# Try this healthy snack

Instead of throwing out bananas that are too ripe, try freezing them. They are a great alternative to ice cream.

---

# Poached Pears    Serves 4

4 Bosch pears, peeled, halved and cored

1/2 cup sugar

1 cup fresh ricotta cheese

1/4 cup toasted walnuts, chopped

4 tablespoons well-aged balsamic vinegar

Combine sugar and 1 cup water in medium saucepan. Bring to a boil over medium heat to make syrup.

Preheat oven to 350°. Place pears in shallow baking dish and pour syrup over pears. Cover with foil and bake about 25 minutes or until tender. Remove from oven, and allow to cool slightly.

Place pears on serving plates, top with ricotta, and sprinkle with walnuts. Spoon any remaining syrup around pears. Drizzle with vinegar over each portion and serve warm.

## Grilled Summer Fruit Dessert

**Serves 6**

2 tablespoons packed brown sugar or Rapadura™

4 tablespoons butter, melted

1/2 teaspoon cinnamon

3 medium peaches, halved and pitted

3 medium nectarines, halved and pitted

2 tablespoons orange juice concentrate

1 tablespoon almond or orange liqueur

1 tablespoon fresh lime juice

Combine butter, brown sugar, and cinnamon in a 9 x 13 baking pan. Add peaches and nectarines. Toss to coat evenly. Arrange fruit in single layer.

Place pan in center of grill. Cook 12 to 15 minutes over medium-to-low heat, until fruit is tender but firm. Turn fruit at least once while cooking. Cool. Cut fruit into thick slices.

In small saucepan, combine orange juice, liqueur and lime juice. Heat through. Toss grilled fruit with mixture and serve warm.

Check out our recipe for Tropical Ice Cream (page 64), a great combination.

## Tropical Ice Cream
**Serves 4**

2 medium-size mangos, peeled, pitted and sliced

1/2 cup sugar

1/2 cup heavy whipping cream

1 tablespoon fresh lemon juice

Fresh mango slices (optional)

On baking sheet, place mango slices in a single layer. Place in freezer for several hours or overnight.

Break mango slices into pieces. In food processor put in broken mango slices, sugar, cream and lemon juice. Process until smooth. Serve immediately or freeze in small serving dishes until ready to use.

### Note from Nancy
Be creative and try this recipe with peaches, bananas, strawberries or apricots. You get the idea.

# Fried Bananas

Bananas
Butter
Maple syrup
Heavy whipping cream

Peel and slice bananas lengthwise. Sauté in a small amount of butter until slightly brown. Transfer to a plate. Drizzle with maple syrup and add heavy whipping cream. Serve while warm.

**Note from Nancy**

This quick, delicious and simple dessert requires very little time. While in Africa, I was introduced to fried bananas. When people take the first bite, there is a silence; they cannot believe it is so good.

# Rich Chocolate Dessert Serves 6

1/2 cup Devon cream, more for topping
1/2 cup whole milk
1 large egg or 2 small
6 ounces bittersweet chocolate, finely chopped

In a small saucepan, combine cream and milk. Bring to a simmer over moderate-to-low heat. In a small bowl beat egg and set aside. Slowly whisk 1/2 cup of the simmering cream into the beaten egg, then whisk the mixture into the cream in the saucepan. Cook for 30 seconds, whisking constantly.

Place finely chopped chocolate in blender and pour in the hot cream mixture. Let stand for 3 minutes. Blend until smooth, about 30 seconds. Pour chocolate cream into 6 serving dishes and place on a baking sheet. Cover and refrigerate until firm and chilled, about 2 hours. Top with a dollop of whipping cream and serve.

**Note from Nancy**

Many types of liqueur can be used to flavor this rich chocolate dessert, especially for dinner parties. We tried adding Marula Fruit Cream, Bailey's Irish Cream, almond extract, and coffee liqueur. They all tasted great, my favorite being Bailey's Irish Cream.

# French Coconut Pie

**Serves 8**
Recipe by Therese Ivey Long

3 eggs

1 stick butter, melted

1 cup of sugar or Rapadura™

1 tablespoon vanilla

1 tablespoon vinegar

1 cup coconut, shredded

9 inch pie shell

Combine these ingredients in a bowl, then pour the mixture into a pie shell. Bake at 350° for approximately 1 hour, checking pie after 30 minutes. Reduce temperature to 325° and bake until golden brown.

**Note from Nancy**

This pie is great fresh out of the oven, but it tastes better the day after it is made. This recipe takes approximately 10 minutes to prepare. Serve with a slice of fresh lemon.

# Fresh Berry Pie    Serves 8

4 cups of blackberries or raspberries
1 1/4 cup sugar
3 tablespoons flour

In large bowl, mix flour and sugar together with hands. Add berries. Set aside.

# Old-fashion Pie Crust

2 cups flour (rounded)
1 teaspoon salt
1 cup shortening
4 tablespoons of ice water

**To make dough for 2 (9 inch) pie crusts:**
Combine 2 cups flour and salt, mixing by hand. Blend in 1 cup shortening, then fold in 4 tablespoons of ice water. Do not overwork the pastry. The less the better.

Divide dough into halves and place on wax paper, sprinkled with flour. Roll with rolling pin, adding flour if necessary. Place pie pan on top of dough and take off wax paper. Press into pan. Cut edges. Use cold water to patch pastry. Punch holes with fork. Bake at 425° until light brown.

Add mixture of berries onto bottom crust. Top with whipped butter and top crust. Bake at 425° for about 15 minutes. Reduce heat to 350° and bake for 45 minutes or until top is golden brown. While pie is still warm, pour on some heavy whipping cream and enjoy.

**Tip:** To prevent spilling, place pie on a cookie sheet lined with foil.

**Note from Nancy**

On my farm I have several acres of wild blackberries, and near my garden I grow raspberries, all organic and all abundant. We freeze many of the berries for the winter, and they make the best berry pies ever.

# Creamy Pear Pie

**Serves 6 or 8**

1 (9 inch) unbaked pie crust
4 cups slice pears, peeled
1/3 cup sugar
2 tablespoons all-purpose flour
1 cup sour cream
1/2 teaspoon vanilla extract
1/2 teaspoon almond extract
1 teaspoon of fresh lemon juice

## Topping

1/2 cup all-purpose flour
2 tablespoons butter, softened
2 tablespoons brown sugar

Pie crust can be baked for about 15 minutes at 400° before adding pear mixture.

In large bowl, toss pears with sugar and flour. Combine sour cream, lemon juice and extracts, and add to pear mixture. Mix well and pour into pie shell.

In small mixing bowl, mix topping ingredients until crumbly. Sprinkle over pears. Bake at 400° for 10 minutes, then reduce heat to 350°. Bake for 45 minutes or until pears are tender.

Pears should be soft, not mushy.

**Optional:** Add 1/2 cup slivered almonds or 1/2 cup rolled oats to topping.

# Sour Cream Apple Pie

**Serves 8**

1 (9 inch) unbaked pie crust

4 cups cooking apples, peeled and sliced

1/2 cup sugar (more or less to taste)

2 tablespoons flour

1 cup sour cream

1 teaspoon cinnamon

2 teaspoons fresh lemon juice

1/2 cup slivered almonds

In large bowl, mix sugar and flour with hand. Add apples, sour cream, cinnamon, lemon juice and 1/2 cup almonds. Mix well and pour into pie shell.

## Topping

1/2 cup flour

3 tablespoons butter, softened

3 tablespoons brown sugar

1/2 cup slivered almonds

In small mixing bowl, mix the topping ingredients until crumbly. Sprinkle over apples.

If you prefer, you can top the pie with a crust and omit the topping.

Bake at 425° for about 10 minutes. Reduce heat to 350° and bake for 45 minutes or until brown and bubbly.

**Tip:** Place pie on baking sheet, covered with foil to prevent spilling.

# Any-Fruit-in-Season Cake

**Serves 8 to 10**
Recipe by Anita Schmidt

1 cup butter

1 cup sugar

6 eggs

2 cups flour

1 teaspoon vanilla

Fruit of your choice

Beat softened butter and sugar until light and fluffy. Beat in 1 egg at a time and continue until well beaten. Then add flour and vanilla. Continue beating with mixer until mixture is thick and mounds up like whipping cream. Pour into greased 9 x 11 inch baking pan. Arrange fruit of your choice over cake mixture. Fresh prune plums are great. You may use fresh peaches, blackberries, raspberries or any other fruit in season.

## Crumb Mixture

1/2 cup butter

1/2 cup flour

1/2 cup sugar

**Cover with crumb mixture:**

Mix butter, flour and sugar together until mixture feels and looks like coarse crumbs.

Bake at 350° or until top is lightly browned, about 1 hour. Serve warm with whipped cream.

# Whipped Cream Frosting

Recipe by Flo Brill

1/2 teaspoon unflavored gelatin

2 tablespoons cold water

1 cup heavy cream

2 tablespoons confectioners' sugar

1/2 teaspoon lemon juice

Pinch of salt

Sprinkle gelatin over cold water in small bowl to soften. Scald 2 tablespoons cream, then pour over gelatin, stirring until dissolved. Refrigerate until mixture reaches the consistency of unbeaten egg whites. Then use egg beater to beat until smooth.

Whip remaining cream. Add sugar, lemon juice and salt. Fold in the gelatin mixture.

This icing stands up even in warm weather.

**Note from Nancy**

For chocolate frosting, omit lemon juice. After folding in the gelatin mixture, add I cup of melted semisweet chocolate chips.

For coffee frosting, add 1 teaspoon instant coffee to cream.

For orange frosting, substitute 1 teaspoon grated orange peel, for lemon juice.

# Sour Cream Cake

1 cup butter, softened

2 cups sugar

1 cup sour cream

2 eggs

1 teaspoon vanilla

2 cups flour

1 teaspoon baking powder

1/4 teaspoon baking soda

1 1/4 teaspoon salt

1 teaspoon cinnamon

4 tablespoons brown sugar

1 1/2 cup pecans

Powdered sugar

Preheat oven to 350°. In large mixing bowl, beat the butter with the sugar. Beat in the sour cream, eggs and vanilla. In a separate bowl, mix the flour, baking powder, soda, salt, cinnamon and brown sugar. Stir these dry ingredients into the batter. Stir in the pecans. Pour into greased and floured Bunt® or tube pan. Bake for 1 hour or until golden. Run a knife around the sides of the cake and turn the cake over onto a cooling rack immediately after it comes out of the oven. When cool, sprinkle with powdered sugar and serve.

**Note from Nancy**

This recipe came to me as a gift from a boy who worked on my farm. This was his favorite cake that his mother made for him. So, he had his mother make one for me. Since that time, I have shared and passed this recipe on to countless friends and family. Now, I am passing this gift on to you.

# Feeding Friends

*best appetizers when you're feeding friends*

My favorite hors d'oeuvres and snacks are included in this section. I like to serve them to friends and family when we gather for conversation, celebration, and good company. The recipes are fast and easy to prepare and reliably delicious. I'm confident you'll find something just right, whether you're wanting savory, spicy, festive, or refreshing.

## Black Olive Dip

1 cup mayonnaise
1 cup sour cream
2 cups black olives, chopped
1 bunch green onions, finely chopped
1 cup chopped fresh cilantro
1/4 cup fresh lime juice
Salt and pepper to taste
2 garlic cloves, finely chopped
1/4 teaspoon of Tabasco sauce or hot sauce of your choice

Combine mayonnaise and sour cream in medium-size bowl and blend. Add olives, green onions, cilantro, lime juice, garlic and hot sauce to taste. Add salt and pepper to taste.

Chill at least for 1 hour.

Serve with fresh tortilla chips.

## Party Peanut Butter and Tomato Hors d'oeuvres

Pepperidge party rye bread
Organic peanut butter
Ripe tomatoes, sliced

Toast rye bread. Spread with creamy organic peanut butter. Top with a slice of tomato and sprinkle with salt.

Serve immediately.

**Note from Nancy**

This is a snack that I eat quite often in the summer when tomatoes are plentiful. I also serve this as an appetizer to guest and friends. This is definitely a unique combination of foods.

# Sunflower Dip

**First layer**

2 (10 1/2 ounce) cans of bean dip

**Second layer**

2 mashed avocados with

2 tablespoons fresh lime juice

**Third layer**

MIX

1 cup sour cream

1/2 cup mayonnaise

1 package of taco seasoning mix

**Fourth layer**

Chopped tomatoes to cover plate

**Fifth layer**

1/2 cup green onions, chopped

**Sixth layer**

1/2 cup olives, chopped

**Seventh layer**

12 ounces cheddar cheese, shredded

(or cheese of your choice)     Place on serving plate in order given, forming a 9-inch circle.

**Note from Nancy**

This dip can be served with crackers or tortilla chips.

# French Baguette

1 pound bacon, fried and patted dry

1 loaf French baguette bread, cut lengthwise

1 cup Gorgonzola cheese (or more if you like cheese)

Dried sage

Cut baguette lengthwise and spread generously with Gorgonzola cheese. Top with crumbled bacon. Sprinkle with dried sage. Place under broiler until lightly brown and cheese is melted.

Cut crossways into finger-size slices and serve.

# Hot Artichoke Dip

1 (16 ounce) can artichoke hearts

2 cloves fresh garlic

1 tablespoon butter

1/4 cup heavy whipping cream

1/2 cup Parmesan cheese

Sauté artichokes and garlic in butter. Add cream, stirring constantly until heated. Add cheese and continue stirring until thickened. Do not boil.

Serve with warm French baguette bread (see recipe above).

# Basil Butter

3 sticks butter, softened
1 1/2 cups loosely packed fresh basil leaves (optional)
Garlic or chives
1 1/2 teaspoons fresh lemon juice
1 1/2 teaspoons white pepper (optional)

In food processor place butter, basil, garlic or chives, lemon juice and pepper. Blend until smooth. Drop by teaspoons onto a cookie sheet and freeze. Remove from freezer and store in freezer bags. Use on French bread. Also great on fish, chicken or vegetables.

# Buffalo Chicken Dip

**Serves 6**
Recipe by Mary Leinmiller

16 ounces sour cream
16 ounces sharp cheddar cheese, shredded
12 ounces Franks Red Hot Original Cayenne Pepper Sauce
4 boneless chicken breasts, cooked and shredded

Combine sour cream, cheese and hot sauce to taste. Add shredded chicken. Place in ovenproof pan and cover with aluminum foil. Bake at 350° for 30 minutes.

Top with crumbled blue cheese and serve with tortilla chips.

This tastes like Buffalo wings without the skin, bones or breading.

**Note from Nancy**

The original recipe called for cream cheese. We substituted sour cream and liked the consistency better.

# Salmon Spread

**Serves 10**

1 pound of smoked salmon

1 tablespoon onion, minced

1 tablespoon horseradish

1 tablespoon fresh lemon juice

1 (8 ounce) package of cream cheese, softened

2 to 3 tablespoons of mayonnaise

1 1/2 tablespoon fresh dill (extra for top)

1/2 teaspoon salt

1 cup sour cream

Fresh parsley

In mixing bowl, combine the first eight ingredients. Mix well. Spread on a serving plate and shape into a loaf. Top with sour cream, fresh dill and fresh parsley. Serve with a variety of crackers. Flatbread is great with this dip.

Great for feeding your friends!

**Tip:** A food processor works well with this recipe.

# Caviar Pie

1 (8 ounce) package of cream cheese, softened
2 boiled eggs, chopped
2 green onions, finely chopped
1 (2 ounce) jar Black Whitefish Caviar
1 fresh lime
Hot sauce (Louisiana Hot Sauce)

With fork, slightly flatten cream cheese on a serving dish (not too thin). Layer evenly with eggs and green onions. Carefully spread caviar on top.

For a kicker, squeeze 1/4 of lime on top and sprinkle with hot sauce to taste.

Serve with unflavored crackers of your choice. (A strongly flavored cracker may interfere with this delicious combination of tastes.)

# Nancy's Protein Snack

This is a sweet, sugar-free, high-protein snack.

3 tablespoons low-fat ricotta cheese

5 drops Chocolate Raspberry stevia

1 teaspoon unsweetened cocoa powder

Heavy cream (just a little)

Mix the ingredients together. This recipe is high in protein with very little carbohydrate.

**Note from Nancy**

Stevia can be purchased at your local health food store or where natural whole foods are sold.

---

# Lemon Grass Tea

**Makes 1 gallon**

8 to 10 stalks lemon grass

4 quarts purified or filtered water

1 quart organic apple juice

Wash and cut lemon grass, leaves and stalks. Place lemon grass and water in stainless steel pot and bring to a boil. Reduce heat and steep slowly for about 1/2 hour. Strain, cool and refrigerate in jar with lid. To serve, mix with 1/3 apple juice, 1/3 lemon grass tea and 1/3 water. Add ice. This tea is very light and refreshing.

**Note from Nancy**

Absolutely one of my favorite healthy discoveries. One afternoon in Africa, friends gathered in the kitchen, and someone began raving about the cook's favorite iced tea. As I sipped her "brew," I was absolutely delighted but didn't recognize the taste. The tea was lemon grass with a hint of apple juice.

I have been making variations of this tea for years and now grow my own lemon grass in my garden. One variation is to add drops of flavored stevia, minus the apple juice. An African original.

# A Reverence for Life

The information that has led to my consciousness regarding health is a result of my continued travel to Africa for over 20 years.

Today, the unsuspecting consumer is ingesting an astonishing amount of chemicals and foreign substances from our food. Some cause an immediate reaction, while others have serious accumulative effects, which are rarely traced to their origin.

While discussing the subject of food, I always find myself expounding on organic healthy eating. I, inevitably, launch into the propaganda we are being fed in this country, from chemicals and pharmaceuticals, to fast food and fat, and greed versus good health. I wind up on my soap box, ranting about genetically altered food and the pillaging of America. So I have decide to put my money where my mouth is. In this cookbook, I've included answers to some of the most commonly asked questions and questions we all should be asking concerning our health and the food we eat.

Most hardcore books on nutrition and health will go so far as to suggest that you should never buy anything in a grocery store. Even though this notion is ideal, it lacks practicality and presents problems for most consumers. I have found that my personal pursuit of good food and healthy eating has not been a challenge, but rather, has been fun, interesting and inspiring. I am fortunate that I have found a true organic market not far from my home. I often trade my art prints for wild organic berries, apples, fruit juices and other homegrown vegetables, and even chicken.

The only way that you can be absolutely sure that you are getting true organic is to buy your food from a local grower whom you trust.

I have joined the growing number of informed people around the world who are questioning the foods that we are feeding ourselves and the ones we love.

—NANCY NOËL

# Whenever possible buy and use organic

## ORGANIC

The definition of true organics: Organic agriculture starts by building healthy soil without the use of chemicals and pesticides, and uses methods that harmonize with nature.

Crop rotation is important in organic agriculture. It helps to reduce the number of pests that affect any one crop.

In non-organic foods, dangerous hormones, chemicals, and antibiotics are passed on to the consumer. These have been stored in the fat cells of living tissues of animals.

History shows us that certain diseases, illnesses and hormonal changes in humans did not exist prior to the use of pesticides, herbicides and the introduction of genetically altered food.

Buying organic is currently the safest way to insure that your food has not been genetically modified. Food that is certified organic must be free of all genetically modified organisms.

The PLU codes (stickers on our fruits and vegetables) inform the consumer whether the produce is conventionally grown, organically grown or genetically modified. Conventionally grown has four numbers (example: 1234). Organically grown always begins with the number 9 (example: 9 1234). Genetically Modified begins with the number 8 (example: 8 1234).

My greatest concerns for the American consumer are trans-fatty acids, food additives, genetically modified or engineered food (GMO), irradiation radiation, and pesticides.

## TRANS-FATTY ACIDS

Trans-fatty acids, commonly known as hydrogenated oils, are the No. 1 killer in our diets and a major contributor to cancer, heart disease and diabetes. Many popular brands of commonly used foods that contain trans-fatty acids include margarine, peanut butter, bottled salad dressing, fast foods, cold cereals, cookies, chips, snack food, lunch meats, cured bacon, frozen meals, frozen pizza, canned gravy, microwave popcorn, cake mixes and many more.

## GENETICALLY ENGINEERED FOODS

Genetic engineering is the technology that allows scientists to transfer heredity information in the form of genes directly from one organism to another. One of the most alarming features of this technology is that gene transfer between species may cause the spread of dangerous diseases across species barriers. Scientists have linked the emergence of disease-causing bacteria, antibiotic resistance, and more virulent viruses to this horizontal gene transfer process.

Genetic engineering has introduced unnatural foods containing bacteria and viruses into our food supply. Unfortunately, genetically engineered foods do not require specific identification on labels. At least 7 out of 10 items at your neighborhood grocery store contain some genetically engineered foods.

What makes genetic engineering particularly dangerous is that no one can predict the new toxins and allergies that will develop as a result of these combinations. Researchers predict irreversible changes in the delicate balance of nature as a result of cultivating genetically engineered food plants.

Genetic engineering has already caused a number of deaths and human illness as well as untold damage to the environment.

> **NOTE:** HOME GARDENERS WILL BE SURPRISED TO LEARN THEY MAY BE GROWING GENETICALLY ALTERED SEEDS UNKNOWINGLY. PLEASE BE AWARE WHEN YOU'RE PLANTING YOUR GARDEN.

Children are especially vulnerable to the vast array of chemicals in food. Many children today are exhibiting symptoms associated with multiple chemical sensitivity.

To learn more about engineered food, we recommend "The Future of Food", a film by Deborah Koons Garcia.

# Have you ever wondered what those pesky little stickers on vegetables and fruits are all about?

## FOOD ADDITIVES

A food additive is any chemical, natural (natural does not always mean safe) or synthetic, that is added during the manufacturing of food. The book *Hard to Swallow: The Truth about Food Additives* will open your eyes to the vast array of dangerous chemicals that are permitted for use in our food supply and will give you a clear understanding of some of the alarming processes used to manufacture the foods you eat every day.

## WHAT IS MSG? (MONOSODIUM GLUTAMATE)

MSG is one of the most commonly used food additives, primarily used to enhance flavor and addict us to certain foods by exciting the nerves in the tongue and brain.

Studies have shown that the consumption of MSG and other glutamates as a food additive causes abnormal function of brain transmitters. MSG has been linked to obesity, Alzheimer's, and Huntington's Disease.

From my research, I have found that this is a far greater problem then most people are aware. If you are interested in more of the research, I recommend the book *The Slow Poisoning of America.*

Some researchers consider the following as "poisons in masks." Always read and check for these additives:

| | |
|---|---|
| Monosodium Glutamate | Hydrolyzed Vegetable Protein |
| Plant protein extracts | Sodium caseinate |
| Calcium caseinate | Yeast extract |
| Hydrolyzed oat flour | Autolyzed yeast |
| Bouillon stalk | Malt extract |
| Glutamic acid | Natural flavoring |
| Monopotassium glutamate | Natural beef/chicken flavoring |

## PESTICIDES

A pesticide is any substance or mixture of substances intended for preventing, destroying, repelling, or mitigating any pest. Pesticides are poisonous to humans and are linked to many types of cancer as well as numerous catastrophic diseases in children, animals and adults.

A pesticide may be a chemical substance or biological agent such as a virus or bacteria used against pests, including insects, weeds, birds, mammals and fish.

*The Shoppers Guide to Pesticides in Produce* lists the 12 popular fresh fruits and vegetables that are consistently the most contaminated with pesticides and those 12 fruits and vegetables that consistently have low levels of pesticides.

| HIGHEST IN PESTICIDES | LOWEST IN PESTICIDES |
|---|---|
| Apples | Asparagus |
| Bell peppers | Avocados |
| Celery | Bananas |
| Cherries | Broccoli |
| Grapes (imported) | Cauliflower |
| Nectarines | Sweet corn |
| Peaches | Kiwi |
| Pears | Mangoes |
| Potatoes | Onions |
| Red raspberries | Papaya |
| Spinach | Pineapples |
| Strawberries | Sweet peas |

Approximately 6 billion dollars a year are spent by Americans on their lawns. Most of the money is for fertilizers, herbicides and pesticides. We have to ask ourselves this question. How is this affecting our water supply? The run-off water of chemically sprayed lawns should be of great concern to everyone.

## WHY WE SHOULD BE CONCERNED

Pesticides can have a long-lasting adverse effect during the critical periods of fetal development, and because the effects of pesticides are not always understood, the shopper should beware.

The best option is to eat plenty of organic fruits and vegetables, therefore reducing your exposure to potentially harmful chemicals. I recommend that you support your local organic farmer and market.

Write your Senator/Representative to strengthen Right to Know laws and to pass legislation to protect the consumer's health.

**ASPARTAME:** The technical name for the brand names NutraSweet, Equal, and Canderel. It is an ingredient in approximately 6000 foods and beverages sold to consumers, worldwide.

Currently the FDA receives more complaints related to aspartame than any other food additive. There are many symptoms and health-related conditions that are linked to the sweetener, ranging from memory loss to brain tumors.

The controversy regarding the safety of aspartame is an ongoing debate and will ultimately be decided by you, the consumer.

For more information, check out the website of Russell Baylock at www.russelbaylockmd.com.

**BALSAMIC VINEGAR:** This vinegar is in a class all its own. It is known for its smooth sweet and sour taste. The finest balsamic vinegar comes from the rolling hills of Modena, Italy.

Balsamic vinegar is great for making your own salad dressings. Be creative when considering the possibilities of using this versatile vinegar.

**BUTTER:** We prefer using butter over margarine for the following reasons:

1. Butter does not contain hydrogenated trans-fatty acids; most margarines do.

2. Butter has been around for centuries.

3. Butter has a better flavor than margarine.

4. It takes 21 pounds of fresh, wholesome milk to make one pound of butter.

5. Butter does contain saturated fat, but some believe that saturated fat may play many important roles in the body's chemistry. They enhance our immune system, they are necessary for healthy bones, they provide energy and structural integrity to the cells, and they protect the liver.

We recommend using organic butter.

For more information on saturated fats go to www.westonapricefoundation.org.

**CLA:** Conjugated linoleic acid, a compound found in many animal fats, is a natural nutrient that may enhance the immune system, prevent cancer and burn fat. CLA are 3-to-5 times more abundant in milk from 100% grass-fed cows.

**COCONUT OIL:** Coconut oil is a colorless-to-pale-yellow oil. It is great for frying and for baking. We recommend using 100% mechanically (expeller) pressed, naturally refined organic coconut oil.

Coconut oil has a long shelf life; it does not turn rancid. Studies have shown that it reduces cholesterol, has antioxidant properties, and also has the ability to stimulate thyroid function. Some believe that it has anti-aging and anti-cancer effects and can aid in weight loss.

**COOKWARE**

Studies have shown that when Teflon (non-stick) cookware is heated to a temperature of 500 degrees F, toxic fumes and particles are emitted. The studies also have shown that at 600 degrees F, the cookware begins to decompose.

These toxic fumes, gases and particles have been linked to the death of pet birds and, possibly, an unknown number of human illnesses every year.

The EPA's scientific advisory board found in 2005 that PFOA a chemical compound used to make Teflon, is a "likely carcinogen."

Consumers who are concerned about potential health risks of non-stick cookware should consider stainless steel or cast iron as an alternative.

Another alternative is anodized aluminum cookware, although some people question its safety, linking aluminum to Alzheimer's.

PFOA is also found in carpeting, food packaging, and clothing.

Recently a class-action lawsuit was filed, claiming the DuPont Company failed to disclose possible health risks of using nonstick cookware.

**FLAXSEED, WHOLE:** Grinding your own flaxseed is one way of getting Omega-3 (fatty acid) in your diet. Store flaxseed in the freezer, grinding only enough for each day. I use a coffee grinder, and it works great. Approximately 2 tablespoons will supply you with a healthy helping of Omega-3's.

### FLUORIDE

A book by Dr. John Yiamouyiannis, *Fluoride: The Aging Factor*, shows that the drug promotes premature aging. He notes that in areas where fluoride is consumed in the drinking water, there are higher rates of bone disorders such as skeletal fluorosis, osteoporosis, and arthritic pain.

He warns that fluoride is a poison. The 1984 issue of Clinical Toxicology of Commercial Products lists fluoride as more poisonous than lead and just slightly less poisonous than arsenic.

To escape the harmful effects of fluoride, Yiamouyiannis suggests buying non-fluoride toothpaste, and not drinking or cooking with city tap water.

Research suggests the most commonly used type of fluoride causes extra lead to escape pipes and ends up in the water supply.

For more information on fluoride, check out, "The Great Fluoride Scam" by James Donahue, on the Internet.

According to reports, fluoride has been discontinued in communities in Canada, the former East Germany, Cuba, and Finland.

Being informed is the key to making important choices for ourselves and our families. There are many pros and cons for the use of fluoride. Please do your homework before deciding to use fluoride or not.

**FOOD ADDITIVES:** Any chemical, natural or synthetic, that is added during the manufacturing of food. Always check your labels.

**FRESH COLD-WATER FISH:** Rich in Omeg-3, good for the heart. Varieties include, cod, salmon, sardines, and mackerel.

**GRAPE SEED OIL:** Grape seed oil is naturally rich in vitamin E (a potent natural antioxidant). This is polyunsaturated oil, rich in linoleic acid. It has a high smoke point, as much as 400 degrees. Great for frying, baking and salads.

**OLIVE OIL (EXTRA-VIRGIN):** As a result of our own research, we have come to rely on olive oil as the principal fat in our diets.

This oil is high in oleic acid (75%), which makes it great for salads and for cooking at moderate-to-low temperatures. Olive oil is rich in antioxidants. Extra-virgin (cold pressed) is best.

**ORGANIC FREE-RANGE EGGS:** These eggs are from chickens that have been allowed to roam in areas where organic grass and certified organic feed is available. They also have chicken coops, which are rotated, for resting and laying their eggs.

**PROTEIN:** Protein is essential for growth and development. Protein provides us with energy and is needed for manufacturing hormones, antibodies, enzymes, and all tissues.

We recommend grass-fed free-range protein. Protein is found in beef, dairy, eggs, chicken and fish, to name a few. The ideal amount of protein in your diet should be about 30%.

**RAPADURA™:** Rapadura is an unrefined natural sugar from evaporated sugar cane juice. It contains its original vitamins and minerals. It is a healthy sweetener and an excellent source of energy. It has a beautiful golden color and a unique Caramel flavor. Simply substitute 1 cup Rapadura for 1 cup sugar.

**RAW MILK:** Raw milk is a complete and properly balanced living food. Raw milk contains beneficial bacteria, enzymes, vitamins and minerals. Raw milk from 100% grass-fed cows is rich in CLA, Omega-3, beta carotene, vitamin E and A.

It also contains lipase, which helps the body digest and utilize butterfat.

**REAL SALT:** Real salt is full of natural trace minerals, including iodine. Real salt contains no preservatives or additives. It is not bleached, kiln-dried, heated or altered with chemicals or pollutants.

**SPLENDA®:** Splenda is not natural; it is a chlorinated artificial sweetener. It is manufactured by adding three chlorine atoms to a sugar molecule. Splenda is found in nearly 3,500 food products. No one can say for sure whether Splenda is safe or unsafe, because there are no long-term studies.

**SPROUTED GRAIN BREADS:** They are 100% flourless breads, made from fresh sprouted grains and are rich in protein, vitamins, minerals and natural fiber.

Consider sprouted grain breads if you are allergic to wheat.

**STEVIA:** Stevia is an extremely sweet, no-calorie herb. It can be sold legally in the U.S., but only as a dietary supplement. It cannot be labeled as a sweetener. Stevia comes in the form of a powder and a liquid.

Most health food or natural food stores carry a wide variety of different flavors, such as Chocolate Raspberry, Orange, Vanilla or, my favorite, English Toffee.

Just a drop or two is all that is necessary. Try it in hot or cold teas or coffee, especially if you want to cut sugar out of your diet.

**TRANS-FATTY ACIDS:** Consumers can know if a food contains trans-fat by looking at the ingredient list on the food label. If the ingredient list includes the words "shortening," "partially hydrogenated vegetable oil" or "hydrogenated vegetable oil," the food contains trans fat. Because ingredients are listed in descending order of predominance, smaller amounts are present when the ingredient is close to the end of the list.

# Thank You's and Acknowledgements

I would like to thank Linda Melick and Sara Slipher for sharing their personal stories, which helped to inspire this book.

I am fortunate to have a certified organic farm, Traders Point Creamery, only a few miles from my home. They have the best eggs, yogurt, milk, cheese and ice cream.

Traders Point Creamery
9101 Moore Road
Zionsville, Indiana 46077
317-733-1700
www.traderspointcreamery.com

Shawn Benzinger is passionate about bringing healthy changes to his patients, coworkers and friends. He believes the human body has the ability to heal itself with the help of spiritual, emotional and physical nourishment. I am grateful to "Dr. B." for teaching me about balance.

Shawn R. Benzinger, D.C., DABCO, FIAMA
3323 West 96th Street
Indianapolis, Indiana 46268
317-872-2989
www.secondopinion.org

**Other Resources**
*Hard to Swallow,* a book by Doris Sarjeant and Karen Evans
*The Future of Food,* a film by Deborah Koons Garcia
*www.meatrix.com*

---

## about the nutritionist

Donna Deardorff, a natural health consultant, has cooked for Nancy Noël for 11 years. In the 1970's, Donna owned and operated her own health food store and restaurant, making her something of a pioneer in the Midwest.

*Dedication*
To my husband, Bob, and my daughter, Crystal. I love you very much.

## about the designer

Jennifer Bradley-Simmons graduated from Indiana State University with a Bachelor's Degree in Broadcast Journalism and went on to study design at the University of Indianapolis. Her work includes many collaborative projects with Nancy Noël, including the print "Spirit of Freedom" and the 2006 release of *The Bedtime Book.* Jennifer also designs a line of greeting cards for Recycled Paper Greetings, Inc., found in Target and card stores nationwide.

*Dedication*
There's more to cooking, and more to life, than a list of ingredients. I dedicate my work on this book to the three strong women who pointed me in the right direction: my mother, Sarah Bradley, my maternal grandmother, Zelma Powers, and my paternal grandmother, Wilma Bradley.